KU-661-354

COMING BACK FROM BABYLON

COMING BACK FROM BABYLON

24 POEMS

Karen Gershon

LONDON

VICTOR GOLLANCZ LTD

1979

© Karen Gershon 1979

ISBN 0 575 02719 3

PRINTED IN GREAT BRITAIN BY
EBENEZER BAYLIS AND SON LTD.
THE TRINITY PRESS, WORCESTER, AND LONDON

FOR NAOMI

ACKNOWLEDGEMENTS

Critical Quarterly, Jewish Chronicle, Jerusalem Post.

"Jephthah's Daughter" was published as a booklet
by the Sceptre Press.

CONTENTS

COMING BACK FROM BABYLON

SARAH

A desert nomad was
Sarah, my ancestress,
and her home must have been
a tent like the Bedouin's.

Oh let me be among,
she must have prayed when young,
the women who bear sons.

Since they feared kings would kill
the Patriarch for her sake
she must have been beautiful.

Her sterile beauty made the desert dance.

II

She walked the desert with the world at stake,
all offspring, small blind creatures made her weep,
oh why, she wept, am I not like the others—
the cry is part of my inheritance,
asking for mercy not for miracles,
all children are born to the death of mothers.

Weeping she walked the desert of God's sleep
and knew his phantasies about the Jews,
Isaac dying through the centuries,
and thinking of his children wept for me,
and with her pity kept his birth at bay.

III

The desert which remade in stone
the pits and pillars of the sun
made God from what it knew of men.

In a camel-coloured tent
Sarah laughed and clapped her hands.

IV

Old age fell from her like the peel of fruit;
a mirage baby skipped across the sands.
Be mine, she called, I'll mother all mankind,
allow me love and I'll be satisfied.
Feeling his fragile skull against her throat
weighted with Auschwitz and Christ crucified
she called, I'm willing! to the desert wind.

JEPHTHAH'S DAUGHTER

I

Knowing her future she went to the hills,
one might have thought it was to meet a lover;
the leaves, the insects whispered to each other,
to die so young and be so excellent!
If it was spring she would not see it ending
and flowers hastened to be where she went.

She stands for my dead sister, for my youth,
for all the sacrifices life demands—
this girl in Gilead who redeemed her father
with frailty more invincible than arms.

II

Since die we must it is a grace
to see the world not slacken pace;
wild things about her called, escape!
At night a lion kept her warm.
She did not argue with her fate,
the nameless girl with my sister's face,
lest someone had to take her place.

III

If she was like myself she made a song.
Oh land, she sang, of orange-groves and palms,
I would have planted vineyards in your deserts
and satisfied Jerusalem with psalms.
And all the birds of Israel about her
agreed to go on singing it without her.

And thoughts of all who died for being Jews,

in wars and at the stake and in the ghettos,
fell out of chaos and became the dew.

IV

While the almond-trees flowered
and the Jordan flowed on
she was like my sister
young and alone.

V

Oh world I love you, she sang to the land,
compared with life, what is a little dying?
In spirit she was like my sister strong.
Be one with me, she heard the land replying;
and still in Gilead when the sap is rising
the hills do homage to her with their spring.

SAMSON IN GAZA

I

They mocked him after he became a slave,
the citizens of Gaza flocked to see him:
the blinded giant with a convict's pate—
for twenty years the Judge in Israel;
they brought their skinny children to feel brave
as they threw stones at Samson in his chains.

Thus Nazi Germany was entertained.

II

He thought, they have my body,
they shall not have my mind,
I will not curse humanity
because of the Philistines;
and he comforted his body
with thoughts of Jerusalem.

III

The sweetest pots we women bake
in the bliss of our wombs
men fill with pride and anger
and sport with till they're ruined.

IV

Such grappling-irons must have come
out of the furnace of his eyes
his captors could not suffer them.

V

One on whose body he had strummed his tune
stood constantly among the changing crowd;
he felt her look and thought it was the sun.
God was no friend, she sighed, when he made man,
we should have been less cruel or less frail.
Long after he was dead, when she was old,
he was still whole and virile in her mind;
but she had loved him better for his wounds.

VI

My father too was made a slave—
God spoils good tools to mend the world;
mourn every hero as a man.
To himself Samson wasn't brave,
I see him with my father's face;
the hands that brought the pillars down
were gentle with his family,
and to one like myself he said,
comfort me.

RUTH

I

Who was that foreign girl who came
destitute to Bethlehem
to be one of Christ's ancestors?

She preferred exile to being alone.

When she stood in the market-square,
in her foreign clothes, of another race,
and was at once surrounded by
her dead husband's family
who knew her by her unknown face—
did she feel, I have come home?

II

She was a stranger even in her sleep:
did not share the language of their dreams;
perhaps one night she tried to run away
—none would have stopped her had she left by daylight—
through dusty alleys to the desert hills,
and saw the sun come up out of her birthplace
and thought it was a sign and felt afraid.
Let me belong, she whispered to the village,
I have come out of death to be remade,
and as the shadows shifted from the valleys
she saw the land as lovely and was glad.

III

I too have chosen to belong
where people see me as a stranger;
I think of Ruth in Bethlehem:

in the childhood of man, was it easier
—before Auschwitz and the crucifixion—
to undo the bonds of race
or did she also feel closer to
past and future generations
than to the people she lived among?

IV

She was a stranger even as a mother:
knew other lullabies and other games;
watching her son at alien rituals
—withholding half of his inheritance
for his sake or because she was ashamed—
she thought, where he belongs I am at home,
and whispered through the prayers of the others,
Oh Bethlehem, my comforter of stone,
oh honey in the desert that is man,
I love you better than I do my own.

ESTHER

I

All the girls wanted to play the queen:
Haman was Hitler when I was young;
but imagine the upstart orphan
in the marvellous palace of Shushan
daring to seek out the king.

II

I'm not alone, she thought, walking alone,
the corridors like harp-strings to her feet,
all those whose lives are threatened are with me,
and saw the mirrors multiply pogroms.

Oh God who raised me put me down, she prayed,
make me suffer but don't make me speak,
you've all mankind and I have only me;
and saw events fall out of memory
—the Jews enslaved, Jerusalem destroyed—
and found an ally in the words to say.

III

Like me, when she was a child
and was hungry and was cold
and the world about her lay
alien with hostility,
she must have heard her elders pray,
return us to Jerusalem,
and seen through green and dancing hills
the dawning of the citadel.

Dressed as the queen and still a frightened child,
God's gamble on compassion between men
—I pity God, she thought, for needing me—
she grew like fire as she hurried on,
her people's fate like brambles to her feet.

Oh choose me wisely for their sake, she prayed,
seeing the millions slaughtered through the ages,
and make me equal to the world you made;
a girl you would have passed by in the street,
who squared her shoulders as she hurried on,
all future acts of courage in her wake.

MOSES' MOTHER

I

Be secret river, the woman sang,
surrendering her first-born child,
and shallow like the heart of man.

She was a slave in ancient Egypt and
it's possible that she was reconciled.
I think she knelt all night long on the bank
and begged and raged and thought of suicide
and cursed God at the coming of the dawn.

II

It happened elsewhere and in other times:
the birth of saviours costs whole generations
—all those expendable babies!—mourned
by mothers who cared nothing for salvation.

III

Small light of life, the mother sang,
my fragile son so finely made,
I am no shelter against fate,
I cast you out because I must;
and still she held him in her arms,
kissed him to feel that he was warm
and once more put him to her breast.

IV

Mankind is like a comet with a tail
of ruined mothers with accusing eyes,
(mine, too, saved me by our separation)

miracle-makers for a little while
when all we know of life is love for us.

V

Replete with a grief so small it cast
    no blemish on the sun,
she held life fast while life itself
    remained indifferent;
God tramples out the stars, she sang,
we are too insignificant,
it's men who do the harvesting of men.

VI

Perhaps the son dreamed of the slip of land
that would enslave mankind's imagination
—oases sprang up where his dream touched sand—
but to the mother it was martyrdom
to let his casket rock out of her hand.

DAVID AND ABISHAG

I

Were there lamps as they lay together,
the village girl and the old king,
after the servants had left?
Wiping her tears like a lover
with his warrior's fist,
he forgot that there had been others
more completely possessed.
They're tears of life, she whispered,
I saw you when you were young.

II

The father of our people, she thought,
    is only an old man,
I'd rather look for a peasant boy
    than stay here as a queen;
but it was the young King David
    she lay with in her dream.

III

In the eyes of the old man
crouched the beauty they had known;
all the bodies they had touched
were bloom on his fingertips;
as the earth has precious mines
he was jubilant within.

IV

I envy God for having thought of you
and life for having loved you for so long

and our land because it is your home
and our people who have served your fame,
the girl's thoughts started singing with the dawn,
I envy our dead who fought for you
and all your enemies who made you strong
and generations harvesting your name.

NOAH ON ARARAT

I

He must have met with silence and horizon:
colours of sky and earth and shades of green
—green fire comforting the chastened earth
nowhere higher than mere days of growth;
nothing stirred between him and the tide.

Where are the birds? he thought into the silence;
he thought, I am like Adam the first man.
The last, the vegetation answered him.

And only then he visualised the violence,
the corpses putrefying in the water,
the earthworm suffocating in the mud.

II

His only weapon was a little scream
lost in the screaming of the lost creation,
God I don't want to have survived, he screamed,
to be alone, to be your memory,
to provide you with other generations,
my sons to kill and to be killed in war;
they were not perfect, oh my friends and neighbours,
but they were not as evil as your slaughter.

III

The earth lay abject in its wealth before
the population streaming from the ark
and everything with wings at once took flight,
mopping the final moisture from the air
until both land and sky were flower-bright;

27

to live, to live, what breathed sang to the hour,
with life as unremembered as the light.

IV

A shabby leader ageing in the sun,
the babies of the ark about his feet
—God's hostages, he thought, who succoured me—
he looked at life and saw that it was young,
was bloody because it was newly born,
a bit of chaos troubled into form—
and followed when the others urged him on.

TOWARDS BABYLON

I

And did they not sing songs of home
trudging towards Babylon?
A population on the move,
almost the whole of Jerusalem:
any column of refugees
must resemble those exiled Jews
—treasure-trove among the nations—
mourning what they would not lose,
burdened with survival and
all they carried and left behind,
every life threshed out to be
another grain of history.

II

The hill was worn from where they caught
a last sight of Jerusalem;
the name would have meant nothing if
the world had not taught Jews to mourn.

III

Imagine them filling the landscape at night:
camp-fires sparking in the desert wind,
the lamentations where someone had died,
and somewhere children's voices raised in song
rejuvenating their inheritance;
I too sat singing there when I was young.

Perhaps some of the Babylonian guards,
sick of the messy after-pains of war
—long absence honeying their families—

sought out the orphans to be sold as slaves
and told them, you will be like our own,
offering homes instead of memories;
and all those persecuted through the ages,
still buds in Eden, shouted out, belong!
The children could not hear them for the song.

THE SACRIFICE OF ISAAC

I

A man who could not tolerate his sons,
the first cast out, he took the other one
to give him like a pagan to his God
(as God gave Christ, having cast out the Jews);
he strode before the boy he hardly knew
—a patriarch who had befriended kings—
as if to do an ordinary thing.

II

And Sarah watched them out of sight
as the womb gives up green bones;
the morning kept the chill of night
the dew stayed on the stones,
and in the desert of the day
the shadows did not go away.

III

Plump with growth were the limbs of the victim,
like a lizard's tongue were his eyes,
he still had on him the bloom of creation
—dry was the wood for the sacrifice.

IV

The hills arose to jubilate
when God declared Jerusalem
and vegetation sprang like deer
from Eden to bejewel them
—and slunk to make the jungle when
it heard what it would witness there.

V

They carry their stakes and they dig their graves
and they die defending merely their lives:
the only river Jerusalem has
is the flow of Jews who are sacrificed.
Oh kill me and save the ram for Christ,
the boy called out as he looked down the ages,
seeing his kinsman nailed to the cross
the centuries streaming from his side,
and fought his father when he unbound him
who thought that it was for the ram he cried.

OUT OF EDEN

I

Once out of Eden they began to age:
change God created when he punished man
and thought up death to be alone again
and then thought it absurd to waste the world
and, dreaming elsewhere, to be done with him,
let man be god enough to create man.

II

Eve pregnant went about the world
in search of creatures giving birth,
not knowing it she mothered them;
and every baby was the first.

III

Mary was not as alone
as Eve was giving birth to Cain;
gazelles and tigers did not come
to the crib in Bethlehem;
gentle both were and ignorant
of their sons' significance
and the love they had for them was the same.

IV

When she had daughters Eve discovered song.
Sweet replicas of me, she sang, be strong,
you are too vulnerable for too long!
not knowing what it was like to be young.

V

Imagine children playing where
primeval forest was before;
the sun shone faster for their sake;
and animals in Paradise
stood by the fence like prisoners
God looking through their eyes.

VI

All Eden heard Eve singing at her chores.
God blessed me with his punishment, she sang,
and gave a purpose to me who had none!
and felt absolved and pitied her no more.

COMING BACK FROM BABYLON

I

When they came back from Babylon
—children of the captivity,
Jerusalem standing in their hearts—
and saw the burned and broken stones
—foxes in the sanctuary—
and under beams and cooking pots
clothing around skeletons,
they stroked the desert dust aside
and as if praying said, we're home.

II

The elders mourned, remembering
       Jerusalem despoiled,
but the young laughed at their labour
saying, bless old Pharaoh
       who taught us to build.

III

At night we walked about the ruined city
—the starlight set out before we were born;
following my parents' memories
I found the house—but every house was home.
And suddenly the stones stood up again
—there were people everywhere—we were besieged—
I smelled the burning and I heard the cries
and saw the casualties and felt the pain.

Let others build their lives, they said,
    we build Jerusalem;
to outlast our enemies
    we build with more than stone.
One drop of blood all Jews gave up:
    they did not build alone.

LOT'S WIFE

I

My home, my lovely home, she wept
while God was sharpening his shafts
against the cities of the plain.
My mother too was called at dawn
and for me Lot's wife has her face,
the same companionable hands
touch what they shall not hold again;
it was because it meant her life
that she was loath to leave that place.

And while her daughters were already running
she stayed to look at a familiar sight:
flowers responding to the early sun
—the valley emulated Paradise;
sweet view, she sighed, if I could leave my eyes . . .
no one will love you after I have gone.

II

What was she doing, waiting there
with darkness spattering the air;
don't hang your hearts on things, she'd said:
a nomad used to moving on
with only a shabby, a makeshift home
and daughters who still needed her
hurrying ahead?

III

I'd be content with yesterday, she thought,
her memories like clothing in her hands:

37

her daughters small, herself reckless and young,
and Lot her shelter, and their wanderings.
If God must take, she thought, let him take all . . .
and shivered as the ground began to shake.

BABY MARY

I

When did the choice of her begin,
was she marked out when she was born,
Jesus shining from within
the baby on her mother's arm,
or was she like her sisters and brothers
to anybody except her mother?

II

Men worship the invisible
—the mother sang a lullaby—
my temple is this miracle
so fragile in her tyranny.
Nothing the corn knows in the seed
of the hunger it shall feed;
little Mary, be my bread.

III

No more than trees that give their fruit
can mothers do, the woman thought,
kissing the pollen from the skin.
I cannot spare her anything
for all the care I wrap her in.

IV

A well in the desert is my daughter,
King Solomon's ships she is to me;
I have a hosanna in my cradle,
sang the woman in Galilee.

V

From all the earth, from all of time
thoughts of people must have come
like gifts to make that baby strong.

MILK AND HONEY

I

Those who were children in the wilderness,
future soldiers and the sons of slaves
—you'll be God's gardeners, their mothers said—
have-nothings, became scavengers of words.
If one began, When we came out of Egypt . . .
they were like livestock at a water-hole.
They tamed the desert with the things they heard.

II

Having kept vigil for the spies' return,
they were the front-ranks squatting at their feet;
they saw the pastures flowering with meat
and fruit like coloured lanterns in the trees
and giants guarding their inheritance;
but they could not imagine so much green.

They did not stay to hear the arguments;
they called out, milk and honey, like a name,
they called it out till it became a chant,
and while their elders shouted, back to Egypt!
the words took hold of them and made them dance.

III

Imagine them grown gaunt with deprivation,
imprisoned in the furnace of God's hand,
until there was a whole new generation
for whom the desert nomads' tents were home.
Still they said, milk and honey, to each other:
a password meaning, we shall reach that land.

RACHEL'S DEATH

They were not very different from us.
When Joseph cried all night long for his mother
—too young to understand that she was dead—
a woman like myself who held him close
whispered to him, love your baby brother.

To get some light she opened up the tent
—that desert view would become Bethlehem—
and felt her breath snatched by the browsing stars.
Perhaps she prayed, Great Shepherd, if you are,
let me atone for what you did to them.

II

Barefoot he squatted beside the baby.
When he fed Egypt and was alone,
all the treasure of the Pharaohs
was dross by comparison.

III

Sundry mothers in the tribe
nursed the baby while the boys
held each other with their eyes.

Repetition makes a rope
of the gossamer of touch;
the new-born did not miss her much.

IV

Out of the granaries of grief

Joseph provided for his mother
as none of us with equal love
have for those who gave birth to us:
an oasis of compassion
where all children mourn together.

I

When they showed him the child he roared with laughter
—all others had been beautiful and strong,
Does this do justice to my greatest passion?
Is this her homage to a warrior king?
and saw their hooded eyes like snuffed-out candles
and muttered, but the boy has done no wrong.

II

Are you so tame, he taunted death,
        that you must feed on crumbs?
Tell God to find me enemies
        and let you feast on men!
But he was on that battlefield
        where none is champion.

III

Hands that had caressed and killed
held the baby patiently;
he thought, what good is my crown to me,
they call me the father of Israel
and I can do nothing for my own child.
The little God asks is all he has;
an early death is a stopped-up well
and he might have watered the wilderness.

IV

Hushed were palace and city
        while the king was shut up alone,
for seven days and seven nights

he prayed to save his son,
and the dust came out of the desert
to darken Jerusalem.

v

I have lost my war with death, he said,
    should I now war with life?
It makes no difference to the dead
    whether or not we grieve,
and clapped his hands for the servants
    to bring him wine and meat.

INTO EGYPT

Trading in spices, once they bought a slave;
not something they remembered and retold,
but into Egypt was a longish way.

They must have made sure he would not escape.
Roped to a camel by his wrist or waist,
was he their equal or an animal;
did one abuse him and another say,
he will recover and can still be sold?

II

Bold were the stars like the eyes of his brothers,
far were his dreams like his father's tents;
night herded child and strangers together
as the desert stampeded before the wind.

III

Perhaps they tamed him as they went
with stories of huge monuments,
water as wanton as the sun
and green fur covering the plain
and towns exuberant with men.

IV

Later, they liked him better than their own:
a mascot with sweet pastures in his head;
I see him burning, bird-boned, gently bred,
beguiling twenty brigands with his dreams.
Perhaps they had agreed to take him back

46

—a motherless boy who made them feel strong—
and outside Egypt told him, stay here, wait;
but he had found his footprints on the track:
his children's children going the other way,
and like a prince bid them, take me along.

THAT NIGHT

I

That night they waited shut inside their houses,
fully dressed and their belongings packed;
small children lay where sleep had caught them up,
older ones watched their parents being afraid.
And then it came: a brief scream far away,
and then another, closer, and another;
a youngest child—my ancestor—exclaimed,
if they don't see the sign they'll kill my brother!

II

Where the angel went that night
the houses became loud and light;
in the slave part of the town
they stayed dark and without sound.

III

I think my mother would have said,
not at the cost of so much blood;
we shall remain the slaves of life,
better the suffering we know . . .
and would have been content enough
to weep that it was time to go.

IV

If we had been the children there
—we too went to the school of death—
we would have gone where Moses was,
enticed from our families

by promises that needed us;
we would have been his messengers.

v

In that night slavery passed like a storm;
and still, to raise what had been beaten down
needed a lifetime between dusk and dawn.

DAVID AND GOLIATH

I

Two hillsides-full of fighting men
sheathed their swords and squatted down,
grinning, to be entertained.

Even among the enemy
some did not want that fight to start;
his brothers had to be restrained.

He wasn't much to keep apart
two armies seething like the sea.

II

His mother did not think of him
as the Psalmist and future king
but as little and quick to cry,
one with imaginary fears,
the baby of the family
with scabby knees and dirty ears
and still in need of mothering.

III

You both look small in the sight of God,
sang the brook to the boy picking stones;
the water that yields to your hand
makes wadis when it is in flood;
you took on the world when you were born,
you can be a giant without big bones.

He must have thought that victory complete:
manna of peace falling throughout the land
and no man dying until he was old,
during that hush before the roar began:
one army fleeing and one in pursuit.

CAIN

I

What made me think he did not grieve?
He killed his brother and left home;
the wilderness took back his fields,
his parents thought of other sons;
he had nothing and was alone.

II

All things looked at him with his brother's eyes,
the younger one to whom he was the source;
all creatures he encountered went in pairs,
the stronger as dependent as the other;
the echo of his senses was, his brother.

III

Gentle must have been his hands
coaxing produce from the land,
that could be so violent.

IV

All the slow builders, time and men,
are quick to destroy;
only what is over remains
unchanged, perpetually.

LEAH

How could she, lying nightlong in his arms,
have fooled her bridegroom with her sister's name?

He must have known his Rachel was not this
reluctant body with averted face
stampeded into passion by a kiss.

For seven years, dull in her sister's shade,
her love had been about him like a slave.

All night she dithered between dread and bliss.

II

She wasn't of those for whose sake
the oceans cleave the continents
and miserable men are brave
and pregnant women count the days
and ecstasy bides in the skin.

III

Warm from her bed he went where Rachel wept.
She picked up garments he had shed in haste,
six tribes in her and barren in the heart.
With such a margin has the world been made,
her lavish love is lost among the waste.

URIAH THE HITTITE

I

Straight out of battle to Jerusalem,
God's promontory with the feel of home
—children at play and old men gossiping
and miracles like bunting in the streets—
he came, one of King David's mighty men,
with quickened eyes and music at his feet.

II

They were waiting for him, his cinnamon girl
and, blinding him like sunshine, the young king
—who would have gone unnoticed in a crowd;
exhausted, grimy, thinking of war he stood
friendless before his best-loved enemies.

III

On wings the day rose as he parted from
the shepherd city dancing through the hills,
the warrant for his death against his heart;
the road rolled up behind him as he went
and in a distant fortress the blithe sun
gilded the sword by which he would be killed.

SAUL AT EN-DOR

I

Who leads the leader? the king exclaimed,
his army outnumbered, war declared,
God silent and his prophet dead.
He laid his royal cloak aside
—and was at once like other men—
and secretly, disguised, by night,
sought out what was lying in wait for him.

II

Not with tree stumps but the dead
was that hill afforested;
dew-ponds mirroring the moon
were the eyes of his three sons;
loudly went the Philistines:
their trophy was his cloven head.

III

The kingdom's greatest warrior stood
abject in the witch's hut
and saw the spectre of her look.

IV

Head and shoulders above his men
he went into battle and was brave;
not any hope of victory
but being human drove him on.